crescendo | decrescendo

poems

bo niles

Finishing Line Press
Georgetown, Kentucky

crescendo | decrescendo

ACKNOWLEDGMENTS

The following poems were previously published: Being him, in
Earth's Daughters, issue #86; U—a dictionary poem, deriving
U words from pp. 1374-1375 of Mirriam-Webster's *Collegiate
Dictionary*, 11th Edition, in *Bluestem* (nominated for a Pushcart
Prize, 2014); and Extinction, in *Bearings*, a publication of the
Collegeville Institute, MN. A longer version of Etude, in *Heart's* issue
#5, was that journal's first-prize winner in 2010; Etude, The Duke
& Dad, Portage and Vespers are in the author's chapbook, *intimate
geographies*, and Extinction, *in natural causes*, both from Finishing
Line Press. In the Jewish tradition, the number 18 signifies 'life'; I
dedicate Eighteen hesitations to my 92Ypoetry group, with thanks
to poet Frances Richey as facilitator.

Publisher: Leah Maines
Editor: Christen Kincaid
Cover Design: Bo Niles
Author Photo: Kara Flannery

Printed in the USA on acid-free paper.
Order online: www.finishinglinepress.com
                    also available on amazon.com

Author inquiries and mail orders:
Finishing Line Press
P. O. Box 1626
Georgetown, Kentucky 40324
U. S. A.

Table of Contents

I—c r e s c e n d o

II—d e c r e s c e n d o

for my sisters
Wendy Thorne Forsyth
and
Candace Thorne Canton
&
to the memory of our father
Francis Burritt Thorne, Jr.

I

crescendo

Etude

In the deckle-edged, sepia-tone photograph
my father hunches over an upright piano
in a pair of bathing trunks,
his fingers blurry where they strike the keys,
his sun-bronzed shoulders—pointy-bladed, splayed—
as tender as the drawn-back wings of a dove,
every knob on his fourteen-year-old spine lit by sun.

He leans hard into the music, his head thrown back,
angled toward the camera, eyes closed tight,
lips hard, I imagine, with humming—
when he plays the piano he always hums—
his only armor his raw eagerness
for the boogie-woogie, rag and show-tunes
his father plays so well.

As he plays, he mimes his father's syncopations
hoping for a word—a glance even—
of his father's sincere regard,
much as Donatello's bronzed and youthful David,
naked but for boots and helmet leafed with laurel,
leaned upon Goliath's mammoth sword
awaited benediction from his Lord.

Behaving like a jellyfish

Years ago, we lived alongside a saltwater creek
that fed into the wider waters of a bay.
Summer weekends my dad motored us out
on his beloved *Sanderling* to picnic on board

and swim. My mother often swam naked.
Spellbound, my sisters and I leaned
over the gunwales to watch her thread her way
among the jellyfish which proliferated

in the bay's tepid waters. Young then,
we girls were capable of believing anything—
that our mother would never get stung,
that our parents would never grow old,

that we would never move away.
Back then, everyone we loved lived nearby.
Back then, we couldn't believe
that anyone we loved would ever die.

There's one type of jellyfish called immortal.
It never dies, but simply grows younger
and younger, then starts its life all over again.
Re-creating its cells is its secret, seawater

the unruffled habitat that sustains it—
just as the miraculous swell of recall
regenerates the memory of our finally
jumping into the water and away

from our dad who waved at the three of us
as we swam through the sashaying jellyfish
to our laughing mom so many years ago.

Aboard

TO SET OFF from our dock on Dad's *Sanderling*
and watch him shift his weight into her wheel
and steer hand over hand with one
of us three sisters locked between his knees
steadying our red Keds on the circular brace
of his captain's chair our hands pushing
the spokes of his wheel with all our might
as we cross Long Island Sound to Fire Island
seagulls rocketing over the vee of our wake

TO FEEL the thrum of *Sanderling*'s engine
as we lie on her smooth sun-toasted foredeck
or curled up next to Mum in the stern
on sun-faded red canvas cushions piped in white
like the white cotton shorts we wear
with our red Keds and our blue-striped tees
our American flag whipping in the wind behind

TO WATCH Dad cut the engine, throw out the anchor
and row us ashore in his dinghy, *Small World*,
him at the oars and Mum at the stern,
and the three of us leaning over the bow
with Oswald our black poodle nosing the wind

TO DASH across the dunes spiked with reeds
to the ocean's foamy fringe bubbled by sand crabs,
our footprints mapping tide trails along the beach

TO PASS such a sunny summer Sunday
with Mum and Dad and Oswald

TO WONDER how long we would know such bliss.

The Duke & Dad

The night the three of us were told to stay upstairs
the living room off-limits to little girls in long pink
nightdresses our hair wriggled free of pigtails upstairs so
we'd be out of the way when the Duke arrived in his long
black coat his hair shiny with brilliantine & his sister Ruth
in her big blond wig & some people called 'backers' &
a 'retinue'—how I loved my mother purring that sound:
ret-in-oooo!—all those mysterious people coming to our
living room to hear the Duke play songs for a Broadway
show swinging songs he adlibbed on one of dad's two
pianos & the thrum of laughter & the smoke until we
heard another bounce of a beat a boogie-woogie our
Dad riffing rhythms with the Duke their syncopations
popping through our bare toes as we wriggled our way
down the stairs until we could almost touch the wild gold
triangle of smoky light our mother's laughter tickling us
all over & seeing the great inky shape of the Dukes big
black coat flung over the arm of the sofa along with next
to Dad's best tie & just the edge of my mother's arm in the
sleeve of the pale green silk dress she kept for best when
she went out to dinner with Dad but never imagined as a
night like this when the Duke came into her living room
to audition songs & not to some midtown club like the
club that then hired Dad to play boogie-woogie & jazz &
sing because the Duke told them about how they played
the piano together while my mother laughed & we
tiptoed back upstairs to dream boogie-woogie dreams
not realizing our lives would change completely with Dad
playing the piano & singing & writing music & living in the
music world for the rest of his life.

Off the cuff

a riff on my dad and Frank O'Hara's "I do this, I do that"

It's after 4pm in NEW YORK CITY on a Wednesday, yes, and I'm home after lunch with my sons, yes, on 52nd Street and Sixth Avenue, a couple of blocks from the HICKORY HOUSE where my dad played jazz piano, yes, when I was a kid and me now wondering if Frank O'Hara who was born four years after my dad and also loved jazz and played the piano ever heard my dad play after his workday at MoMA as a curator who wrote poetry on his lunch hour and on napkins and envelopes which I don't and not this on this Wednesday, yes, because I was having lunch with my sons and then went to buy a ticket to a musical coming to Broadway from CAMBRIDGE, MASS. where Frank O'Hara went to HARVARD after working with sonar in World War II like my dad though my dad graduated from YALE *before* his sonar training which I think about just as I think about how I love musicals and my dad not only played and sang Broadway show tunes but he composed serious music too which he majored in at Yale just like Frank O'Hara did at Harvard before he switched to English and began writing poems alongside his roommate Edward Gorey who wrote 84 books like THE CURIOUS SOFA and whereas my dad got engaged to my mom in college Frank O'Hara began to take lovers like the painter Larry Rivers saying "if you're going to buy a pair of pants you want them to be tight enough so everyone will go to bed with you" and "you just go on your nerve" and Frank O'Hara nervy as ever died in an accident in a dune buggy on FIRE ISLAND when he was just 40 years old the month after I graduated college and Larry Rivers wrote his eulogy and just then I realized my dad lived over twice as long as Frank O'Hara and my breath stopped

Firenze 1962

Our rooftop overlooks the old city,
    its terracotta tiles formed
by conforming to an artisan's thighs.
The roof-clay warms us sisters
    as we lie between rows of tiles just
outside our bedroom window
    our arms and thighs humming to the heat
and the beat of our dad's piano
    downstairs as he parses a new composition,
its rhythms as silky as his oar-strokes
    when he rows his single scull out along the Arno
just a few heartbeats away
    from our roof and the shadowed courtyard below
where our mom listens to our dad hum
    out his rhythms as she reads by a cool marble well.

Twin lens reflex

Behind her Mamiyaflex
with its heavy wooden grip
my mother frames the two of us
in a plate-glass window
spelling the word R I S T O R A N T E
in capital letters over our heads,
38-year-old you lanced by the first T
and 16-year-old me between the A
and the N, the two of us
grinning at each other across
the bright white linen tablecloth
with my Coke and your Pellegrino,
my mother's empty chair pulled
away from the table,
away from us
into her
CLICK

Myth

My parents met when they were both 14.
They met because my mom said 'yes'
to going to the movies to five boys—
and one brought along my dad.

I never asked what movie they saw.
I never asked about the other boys.
I never asked because my dad was my dad.
The boy she met when they were both 14,
was engaged to at 18 and married at 20.
The boy who went to war, came home,
was dad to my sisters, my dad to me.
The boy my mom always said was The Only One.

After she died, I brought home an antique box
she'd carried everywhere my parents lived.
Crafted from wood, the box had always stood
on a chest at the end of my parent's bed.
Its cover, inset with an edenic scene, was guarded
by glass, cracked, but never repaired, and hinges
and a keyhole filigreed in metal. There was no key.

When my handyman broke open the box
(at the hinges, nothing would turn in the lock),
out tumbled so many letters from so many boys,
including a packet from a boy named Mo
my sister said my mom was not allowed to marry.
How did she know that and I did not?

I never knew because I never asked.
I never asked because my mom had polished
her story of our dad to flawless perfection.
Dad, the boy she met when they were both 14.
The boy who wrote only two letters in that box.

To my father from Helen Keller

My fingers tap out this message
on your upturned palms
S   O   S
so you may sense how your daughter
sensitizes herself to create
a hallowed space in her heart for you
and then listen:
Listen for the first word that nourished me—
not *Da Da* but *Wa Wa*
this word I offer you as your daughter
begins to root herself in her own oasis
where she may be nurtured
as the world unfolds for her
as yours did with your music
and mine did when water overflowed
the lifelines etched into my palms.

II

decrescendo

An adult life clocked in 12 words
after Robert Irwin:
'seeing is forgetting the name of the thing one sees'

[*lifesource*]
wife

[*the narrows (part l)*]
war

[*the narrows (part 2)*]
daughters

[*the dots*]
piano

[*playing the horses*]
Florence

[*being available in response*]
composing

[*play it as it lays*]
singing

[*down to point zero*]
dementia

[*present all around*]
humming

[*seeing is savoring*]
vigil

[heaven]
prayer

[*afterword*]
tears

Going downhill

At the front desk, he stacks Shopper's Guides so they align.
At the lobby piano, he replays his favorite Gershwin and Berlin.
At the mailbox, he tosses everything into the recycling bin.
At *Let's Read*, he barks 'she made six mistakes again.'
At meals, he dribbles food on a shirt he's already stained.
At his apartment, 33 photos remind him of his Ann.
At his desk, a lined pad tells him what day it is and when
   to do whatever he does which my sister underlines
      with his blue pen which he Xs through
        untileachpageblursintoablobofblue
each page blooming into how he too
is bruised into maybes and nevers and ever since then.

The man who

sharpened his pencils to the precise same length,
lined them up side by side on his desk in a strict and tidy row,
marked his scores so they could be copied note by note,
was the man who said when you asked him why:
I care.

stole mints by the handful from the Country Kitchen,
hid their wrappers behind the curtain in his room,
tossed the half-sucked ones onto the rug under his bed,
and said when you asked him why:
I don't care.

slurs syllables from all those show tunes he can no sing,
barely eats or drinks and can no longer see,
sleeps and sleeps even when I'm there.
Does he care?

This is the man I often, for a long while, didn't care.
This is the man I had to relearn how to love.
This is the man.
Who.

U—a dictionary poem

Unutterable. Unworldly. The up
heaves of yourself from yourself
those sulky outbursts and groans
upset our uncertain universe—
even as a comparable conundrum
presents itself: A glacier up
heaves then sulks and groans
in its efforts to upend continent—
even as the bedrock of you
skids into unearthly dementia.

Erosion

In the brain, 100 billion cells
mirror the granular geography of galaxies,
each synapse linking novas discharging
a vast universe of thought.

Memory claws at the scuffed scaffold of history.

Strike the wrong keys and songs
that had been artful proofs of comprehension

     vaporize
                 and everything
         once
    salted away
backspaces

marooned as an encrusted derangement of erasures
until the one you've been trying so hard to love
     dissolves

      into an unimaginable

            abyss

Extinction

I sense the evidence everywhere: my dad afloat
in his dementia; oceans rising; ice melting,
cracking on stone. Naturally drawn to landscapes—
marsh, desert, rivers, sky—my husband and I stream
a documentary by a filmmaker who bungeed a camera
to an Arctic outcrop where it gazed, unblinking,
at a glacier as it receded, reverted to slag (eons of ice
and rock rasped to gravel within a matter of weeks).
We listen to the bark of calved bergs as they slide
into the sea. We sense the heart-thump of a polar bear
afloat on a ten-foot floe and remember the foot-thump
of another at the zoo as he swam back and forth slamming
his paws against the glass wall of his cage until he died—
like a mangy old rug in a men's club, spread under the feet
of a snowy-maned member, the smoke of a cigar islanding
his head, his graveled voice declaiming the demise
of the great auk while checking if buffalo was still on the menu.
The next day, at a ladies' lunch, *iles flottantes* are wobbled out
on frosted plates. A woman flashes a giant solitaire, laughs.
Global warming, she barks; *You must be demented!*
Where's the evidence of that? Back home there's a message
from my sister: *Dad played* 'How Deep is the Ocean' *today,*
but he couldn't remember the words. He has played and sung
hundreds of songs for us, for eons it seems. How long
will it be before the last one slides into the sea?

Masquerade

He has been moved into the wing they call Gardenside.
It is safe there. An eden of sorts.

Surveillance is key to his new regime: the wristband
embossed with his name; the panic call button
suspended around his neck; the hourly Depends checks;
new slippers; the lock on the outside door to the wing.

Here he plays Bingo with chocolates instead of dimes,
popping them into his mouth before the tally.

No one is awarded a prize at this mock entertainment—
so unlike the Carnivale we loved when we lived in Italy,
which spilled across Venetian canals as bacchanal.

Today, artisans still conjure their alchemies of gesso,
glitter and glass into fantastical masks for the festival.

> Bauta dons a swirl of black cape, a tricorn hat.
> Colombina shoulders an immense shrug of feathers.
> Zahni thrusts out a long leather snout upturned at the tip.

All follow the Plague Doctor, his hands gloved in white.

Oh Daddy,
behind the mask of oblivion that has eclipsed your smile,
are you visited echoes of water-borne music that once
led us on?

On REMOTE

POWER ON how I have prayed to recover you even as I always imagined **RECORD** I would die before you which would **SHIFT/MODE** be so much simpler than trying to follow the **SCAN** of your one good eye as it retracts to a pin dot of blue (so much smaller now than when it **ON DEMAND** used to pierce me to the quick) and now attempts to **SHIFT/RESET/PAUSE** see me now that sight and words fail you   (and words fail me now too) though I try I do I do try to recall   **FAVORITES**   like what you were saying to me in that picture my mother took of the two of us laughing in that restaurant on that afternoon when your life of making music **VOLUME UP** bloomed before you while mine **STOP/REWIND** wobbled on the prayer of your smile reflected in the shimmering window glass **POWER OFF**

Eighteen hesitations

...what I seek is the space between the rain —Agnes Martin

I consider	the morning rain this day
I reconsider	the dimensions of this this day this rain
I remember	the sun from another day
I forget	other days with sun and rain and him
I reconsider	how remembering was once so natural to him
I consider	how remembering could be
I remember	much that was remembered without saying so
I forgive	or do I or can I really
I reconsider	scars can't always check wounds of remembering
I forget	how remembering now surfaces from so long ago
I consider	every scrap of memory must now be monitored
I reconsider	how I could ever have imagined being so vigilant
I forget	how remembering must be so difficult for him
I remember	what
I remember	that now I too do not always remember
I remember	so much now that I don't want to remember
I reconsider	what I might and should remember
I forgive	or try to without remembering only the rain

Vespers

Indian summer has come and gone
leaving earth to retire into reticence
and squirrel her sometime seed
into the antlered armature of a tree.

Leaves dead
*are driven, like ghost*s

rasped to dust, their bitterness plain
their lees after rain as bitter as wine
turned to vinegar in the cask.

Leaves dead
driven
ghosts

like my father's recall which disowns him
along with so many photos interleaved
within albums harrowed as husk.

sitting on the porch, August '41
home at last, 1945

Leaves
driven

photos

ghosts

into a lake whose surface is screed
with a precarious grisaille encrypted
from
cloud

Portage

When day is gone and night comes on ... —*Cole Porter*

the blessed finger-holds
of his piano keyboard
tether him to the handful
of notes
that remain
of his once reverberant world
his fingertips clinging
to what he can barely sing
while we strain

     yearning . . .

through the wavering echoes

     dream dancing . . .

before silence

       little dream . . .

makes a ghost of his song

Before . after

My sister and I are sitting in her car
in the parking lot behind the bank
talking through *before he fell*
and fractured his hip
and the comparative merits
of *after surgery + rehab:*
>   *return to Gardenside?*
>   *transfer into the nursing home?*
when a red fox sashays right on by the car
marking this time between whatever
we decide . . . silencing us
and letting us know that it is not only feral,
but free,
not tethered like our dad to
decisions like ours nor to the belt
held by an aide as he stumbles
behind his new walker humming
some distant Broadway tune
gumming where his teeth used to be

Threshold

All that remains now is thirst—
and the blanks to fill in with love
as our hands hold his, our thumbs
grazing skin over vein and bone.

His hands flutter, a whisper of butterflies,
as he welcomes us with his toothless smile
    oh oh you've come!

then drops into sleep, curled on his left side,
his hip bone tented by a sheet,
his johnny gown sliding off collar bones
as fragile as the dried-out wishbone
we used to pull apart after
he carved our Thanksgiving turkey.

Suddenly his eyes fly wide open:

    We must fly to Florence at once.
      Hurry!

My sister calms him; he sighs, shifts,
and quiets as we whisper to each other
the way we did as girls in the room
we shared back in Florence, and will again
at our inn before we slip into sleep,
each of us curled on our left side,
the side closest to the heart.

Lipsynching Harry Belafonte at 94

To my daughters:
I've lasted longer than I understand.

This is not modesty,
but part of a bigger search for me.

I've often felt there must have been
something I should have done

but did not do—but what that is
I don't know. What have I said?

What needs to be said?
What's missing?

Sestina

1	2	3
you	fear	dream
hope	you	fear
dream	help	sing
sing	hope	you
help	sing	hope
fear	dream	help

4	5	6
help	sing	hope
dream	help	sing
hope	you	fear
fear	dream	help
you	fear	dream
sing	hope	you

Being him

the is of his / was

the was of his / isn't

the isn't of his / is

the will be

him

Haiku

In the almost dark,

The tremor of you shivers.

What are you saying?

Aria

Melody peels away like the skin of a snake.
Stop. Pause the song.
I want that familiar refrain with its rainbow harmonies
to thrill my lungs so that I might continue to breathe
for the two of us. I want to inhale
this coda of your life
so I may attune myself to the sigh of your shadow
before it shrivels under the moon.

Bo Niles is a former magazine editor, photo stylist, and writer who specialized in home design. She has written several books on design subjects, as well as a travel memoir. Her poems have appeared in a number of anthologies and journals, including *Podium*, from New York City's 92nd Street Y, where she is a member of the Himan Brown Senior Center poetry workshop. Finishing Line Press published her two previous chapbooks: *intimate geographies* and *natural causes*.

Francis Thorne, about whom these poems were written, was a jazz pianist, an award-winning composer and co-founder of the American Composers Orchestra in New York. Elected to membership in the American Academy of Arts and Letters and the Century Association, he served on the music committees for both organizations, as well as that of the MacDowell Colony. A champion of the American Songbook, he was picking out favorite songs on a keyboard until the very end of his life.